Conten...

Intro

This is a book about war. It's a war that's been going on for thousands of years. Our enemies are tiny, but they are all round us in huge numbers. They have killed millions and millions of people in every country on earth.

These enemies are **germs**. They are much too small to see, but their effects can be terrible.

The Black Death killed 40% of all the people in Europe in the 14th century. Malaria kills almost half the small children who die in Africa every year. Spanish Flu killed at least 27 million people just after the First World War in 1918.

Scary stuff, isn't it? But don't put the book back on the shelf just yet. It isn't all doom and gloom. (I bet you like a bit of doom and gloom anyway.)

So what's this book about then?

It's about how scientists found out the causes of these terrible illnesses. It's about how they began to find ways to fight back to protect us against the germs.

It's about a war that never ends.

Chapter 1
What Are Germs?

To scientists, there are no such things as germs.

I bet that's surprised you! The things that get called germs in newspapers are mostly either **bacteria** or **viruses** – I'll tell you about that in a minute. There are some other things that get called germs too, but I'm not going to bother with most of them (apart for malaria, which is scary enough to make it into this book – you'll read about it later).

Every living thing is made of cells. You are made of billions of them. **Bacteria** are living things that are just a single very simple cell. Your skin is covered in them and your guts are full of them. In fact, you have more bacteria cells in your body than cells that are actually part of you! Luckily, most of them are harmless, and some of them are very useful. Harmful ones can give you a sore throat, or food poisoning, or kill you with the plague or tetanus.

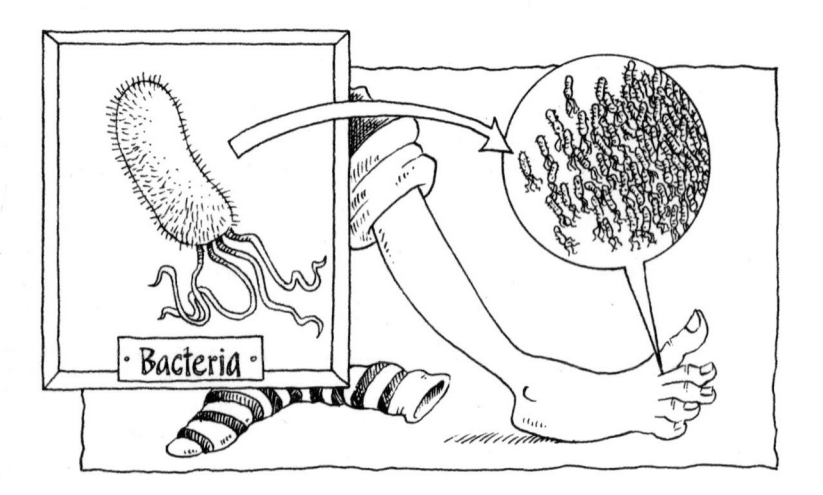

· Bacteria ·

Viruses aren't really living things at all. They aren't cells, just a few instructions inside a bit of protein. They break into cells and take them over, and make them produce more viruses instead of doing what they would normally do. Because they break into the cells, they damage them, and the effects of this damage appear to us as disease. Colds and flu are caused by viruses. So are smallpox and polio, both of which can kill you.

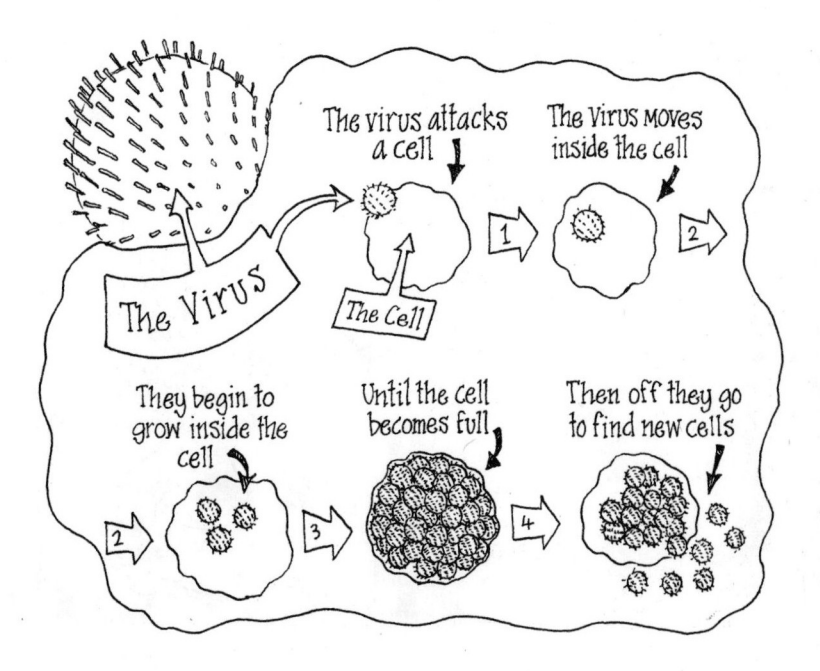

The Virus

The virus attacks a cell
1

The Cell

The Virus moves inside the cell
2

They begin to grow inside the cell
2

Until the cell becomes full
3

Then off they go to find new cells
4

We know now that these germs are what cause a lot of diseases, but until the middle of the 1800s no one realised that. This was because the germs are so tiny that no one knew they existed until the microscope was invented.

Chapter 2

Diseases You Never Want To Meet

The Black Death

Even the name is scary, isn't it?

Black Death (which was also called the plague) first appeared in an island near Italy, called Sicily, in 1347. It spread very fast. There was no cure, and almost everyone who got it died a terrible death. It vanished 350 years later at the end of the 17th century and has never come back. Maybe you sang about it when you were little.

What?

See if you recognise this:

Ring a ring of roses, a pocket full of posies, Atishoo, atishoo, we all fall down.

It's a very scary song once you find out what many people think it means.

'Ring a ring of roses' is said to be the round red rash on your skin that would be the first sign you had the disease.

'A pocket full of posies' is because people used to hold a posy (a little bunch of flowers) in front of their noses to protect them from the Black Death. (This didn't work, of course).

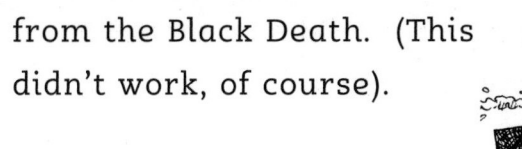

'Atishoo, atishoo' is the sneezing that was an early sign you were ill.

'All fall down' just needs one word added to explain it. Dead!

If you got the Black Death you got the red rash and started to sneeze. Next you got very painful lumps in your armpits and purple spots on your skin. The lumps turned black (which is why it was called the Black Death) and sometimes burst. Once this happened you were definitely going to die. Not for a few days though. In those few days you were in agony, and bleeding inside. All your organs (like your lungs and liver) started to break down into a sort of bloody soup. Some people went mad from the pain and thirst and jumped out of windows or into rivers. It was a terrible way to die.

There was a very bad outbreak of Black Death in London in 1665. It killed 1 in 7 of all the people living there at the time. It was stopped by the Great Fire of London, which burned much of the city, and killed the germs at the same time. A bit drastic, but it worked ...

No one knew what caused the Black Death. Some people said it was God, who wanted to punish them for their sins. Other people thought it was caused by black magic, or poison. They were all wrong, of course.

So what did cause the Black Death? That's an interesting question. I thought I knew the answer until I started writing this book, but now, I'm not so sure ...

It turns out that there are two completely different ideas, each backed by a group of scientists who think they have the right answer.

One group of scientists thinks the Black Death was caused by a bacteria. The same bacteria that caused another disease called Bubonic Plague. They think that Bubonic Plague and the Black Death are the same disease. Bubonic Plague can still be found in some countries. It kills rats as well as people, and it's spread by the fleas that live on the rats.

The other group of scientists thinks Black Death was caused by a virus that died out when Black Death vanished in the 17th century. If a virus kills almost everyone it infects, in the end it runs out of places to live, and dies out itself. (There are other deadly viruses like the Black Death still around in Africa and Asia though.)

Both groups of scientists are sure that they are right. It's amazing to think they still haven't made their mind up about something that happened more than 500 years ago.

Spanish Flu

You might have had flu. It makes you feel really ill. It's much worse than a cold. But unless you're already ill or very weak, it won't kill you. Spanish Flu was different though. It appeared all over the world just after the end of the First World War in 1918. No one knows for sure how many people it killed. I've read figures that say anything between 27 million and 40 million.

No one knows where it started. It doesn't seem to have been Spain, in spite of the name. Most new types of flu start in Asia, often in China. The very bad ones tend to be viruses from birds like ducks, that change just enough to be able to live in humans. Scientists worry that this might be starting to happen again now. That's why there are often stories about Bird Flu in the news. We have more medicines now that might help if a deadly flu appeared, which is good. But we have air travel now, which is very bad, because it could spread all round the world very quickly. Let's just hope it doesn't happen ...

Smallpox

You won't ever have met anyone who has had smallpox. Hopefully, you never will. It's the only living thing in the world that humans have killed off totally, on purpose.

Be very glad it's gone. It was an awful disease. If you got it, you came out in horrible spots and had a very high temperature. 1 in every 3 people who caught it died from it. If you lived through it, you would be left with very bad scars from the spots. It was also very easy to catch. You could get it by touching someone who had it, or even by breathing the germs in, just like catching a cold. This meant that once it started somewhere, lots of people would get it.

The story of how we learned to protect ourselves against it is a bit further on in this book.

Malaria

If you've heard of malaria, you probably think it's an illness you only get in the tropical bits of the world. You're right just now, but a few hundred years ago, you could have got malaria in some parts of England. Scientists are worried that this might happen again if global warming makes things heat up.

Malaria is spread by some types of mosquitoes (a small biting insect). It's one of these things I talked about earlier that isn't a bacteria or a virus. It's a single celled living thing (it wouldn't be right to call it an animal) that lives in mosquitoes' saliva glands, but doesn't make them ill.

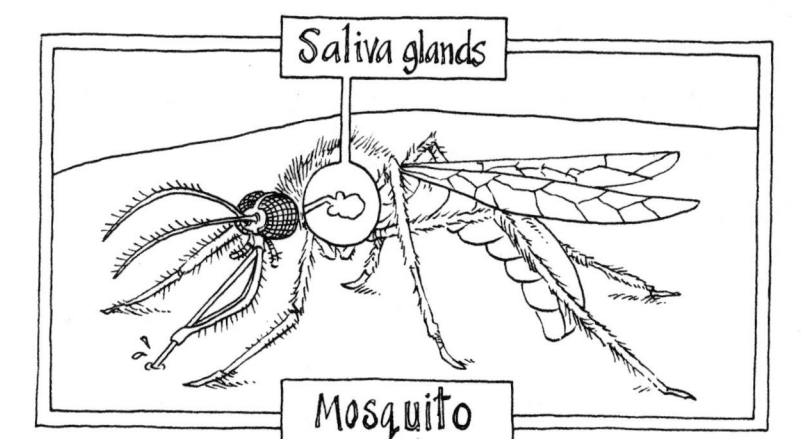

Saliva glands

Mosquito

If it gets into a human though, it gives them a very high fever which goes away and comes back, over and over. If it's not treated with the right medicine it can damage the kidneys and the brain, and you can go into a coma and die. It infects between 300 million and 500 million people every year and kills about 2 million, many of them children. Malaria has played a big part in many wars.

In the American Civil War, which lasted from 1860 to 1865, more than 50% of soldiers caught malaria each year. 10,000 soldiers died from it.

In the early 1800s the French leader, called Napoleon, had large areas of land in Holland flooded so that mosquitoes would breed there. As a result, more than half of all the British soldiers who were trying to fight the French in the area got malaria.

The treatment wasn't much fun either. You might be given medicine to make you be sick, or the doctors might cut one of your veins open and let you bleed for a while. (This method was used to treat all sorts of illnesses in those days. Completely mad, of course.) If this didn't work they would try pouring cold water all over you or try burning your skin. I'm sure I don't need to tell you that none of this did any good at all.

Even if you weren't ill when they started, you would be when they finished ...

We still don't have any very good treatments for malaria. There is no vaccine, but there are drugs you can take if you're going to an area that has malaria. These make it harder for malaria to infect you.

The best way to try and prevent it is to kill the mosquitoes, the insects that carry malaria. You can do this either by using chemicals to kill them, or by draining ponds and marshes where they lay their eggs, but it's not easy.

Anthrax

In 1942, British scientists put some sheep on a tiny Scottish island called Gruinard. Then they blew up a small bomb near them. They weren't trying to blow the sheep to bits, and none of them were hurt in the blast, but a few days later they were all dead anyway.

The bomb was filled with anthrax bacteria, and the scientists were testing it to see if it could be used against people, not just sheep, in the Second World War. It was never used as a weapon though, which was a good thing. We'll come back to what happened to the island of Gruinard in a minute.

Anthrax is most common in sheep, cows and pigs. They pick up the bacteria on grass as they eat. Humans can catch it if they handle sick animals, or eat them. They can also be infected by the skins or wool of sick animals. Luckily, humans can't pass on anthrax to each other.

If anthrax gets into you through a cut, you have a 20% chance of dying. If you breathe it in however, and it gets into your lungs, you will almost certainly die. The bacteria become active, and produce loads of new anthrax bacteria, making it very painful to breathe. The bacteria produce a poison, and also damage your blood vessels so that you can bleed to death internally.

Treating people with lots of antibiotics helps. But only if it's done quickly. Antibiotics are medicines that we use to kill bacteria. There's more about them later in the book.

There is a vaccine, but you need 6 lots of it to stop you getting anthrax, and it's pretty painful, so you wouldn't be given it unless there was a good reason. Soldiers are sometimes given it if they're fighting where anthrax might be used as a weapon against them.

The thing that makes anthrax really nasty is that the bacteria can form things called spores (a bit like seeds) that can survive in soil for many years. Maybe hundreds of years. They could be out there waiting for you now ... (It's not that likely though, so don't worry too much.)

That brings us back to the Scottish island of Gruinard.

After the anthrax bomb was set off, barbed wire and warning notices were put all round the shore, and no one was allowed onto the island for almost 40 years. In 1986 a company was paid to make the island safe. They treated the whole place with a chemical that's supposed to kill the spores, and took away tons of soil. (I wonder where they put it?) Sheep were put on the island to feed on the grass to show it was safe. In 1990 the warning signs and barbed wire were taken down.

Is it really safe though? In other places anthrax spores have been found that are still alive after hundreds of years. I don't think I'll be booking a holiday on Gruinard just yet!

Germ Warfare

Germ warfare (sometimes it's called biological warfare) is a very horrible way indeed of trying to kill people. It means using germs, maybe in bombs, just like they tested on Gruinard. Lots of countries round the world have tried to make germ weapons, even when there are agreements between countries not to have them. Just think of some of the diseases I've described being spread on purpose ... It's just too horrible.

You might think germ warfare is fairly new, because bombs haven't been around for all that long, but armies have used germs as weapons for thousands of years. Ancient armies used fungus to poison the water in their enemy's wells to make people ill and confused. Roman soldiers used to throw dead bodies of animals and humans into their enemy's water supplies or over the walls of a town. The germs that made the bodies rot could make people that drank the water ill.

One army in Russia in 1346 threw dead Black Death victims over the wall of a city. Lots of the people in the city then got the plague too.

In America in the 1700s, the British army gave American Indians blankets that had been used by people with smallpox. Hundred of Indians died as a result.

In the First World War a German secret agent living in America grew anthrax. He used it to infect thousands of horses that were being sent to France to help in the war. Many of the animals died, and they also infected hundreds of soldiers with anthrax.

Since 1972, biological weapons have been banned in most countries, though some countries may still make them in secret.

Chapter 3
Fighting Back

Deadly Hospitals

Hospitals used to be very dangerous places. If you went into one ill, you would probably come out dead.

This was because no one knew what the cause of diseases like blood poisoning was, so no one knew what to do to prevent them.

If a doctor had to carry out an operation, he did it in his normal clothes. He didn't wash his hands before the operation, (though he would wash them afterwards so he didn't get blood on his clothes!)

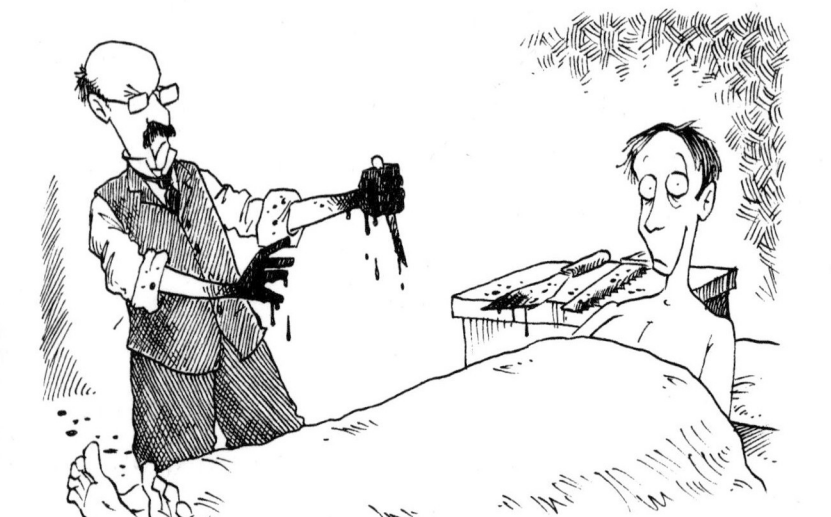

It wasn't until 1847 that a Doctor Semmelweiss, who worked in a hospital in the city of Vienna in Austria, started making his students wash their hands in between touching dead bodies and treating ill people! I'm sure you won't be surprised to know that the death rate dropped from 20% to 1% among the people they treated when they did this.

Most other doctors at the time thought that washing your hands before treating people was a very silly idea. This was because no one knew yet what caused these sorts of diseases. It was 1864 before a French scientist called Louis Pasteur proved that bacteria and viruses are to blame. Suddenly, washing your hands made sense.

Disinfectants

"Oh, come on," I can hear you say. "How boring is this going to be?" Not at all, I hope.

Imagine you live in the 1800s, and you've just been told that your leg has to be cut off.

"Don't worry," says the doctor. "You won't get blood poisoning and die. We're going to put hot tar all over the stump that's left when we cut your leg off."

"Oh, good," you say. Or perhaps you don't.

Anyway, that's what they used to do when someone got an arm or leg cut off, to stop it going bad. Hot tar, just like they put on roads.

Now, I would love to know who came up with that idea, and what made them think of it. I mean, it's not the first thing you think of is it? It's hard to imagine a doctor saying, "I know! We'll try putting a bit of that stuff they use on roads on this man's leg. That's bound to help. Make sure the tar's nice and hot."

A Scottish doctor called Joseph Lister made up his mind to find out why tar helped. One of the things in tar is carbolic acid. Lister tried to spray this onto wounds after operations, and soaked bandages in it. The carbolic acid stopped wounds going bad, but it also stopped the wounds healing. Lister had to do lots of experiments to find the right strength of acid to use so that it would kill the bacteria that were making the wounds go bad, but still let the wound heal.

Carbolic acid was the first disinfectant, and no one had to dip themselves in tar any more.

(Even when I was little though, people still used to go and sniff hot tar if there was a road being mended. It was meant to be "good for your chest." Ask your grandparents, and I bet they'll know what I'm talking about.)

Edward Jenner and Vaccination

Edward Jenner was born in 1749 and worked for most of his life as a country doctor in England. There was an old story in Britain at that time that milk-maids (girls whose job it was to milk cows) had lovely skin and never got smallpox. They often caught a much less nasty illness called cowpox from the cows they milked though.

Jenner wondered if getting cowpox made it less likely that someone would get smallpox. In 1796 he made up his mind to carry out an experiment to see if he was right. This wasn't just any experiment though. If it had failed, he could have been hanged for murder!

Cowpox and smallpox both give you blisters full of goo called pus. Jenner took some pus from a cowpox blister on the hand of a local milk-maid called Sarah Nelmes. She had caught cowpox from one of the cows she looked after. (The cow was called Blossom. Isn't it amazing someone made a note of that?)

Jenner got an 8-year-old boy called James Phipps to let him experiment on him. (Now, I know 8-year-olds are pretty daft, but not normally that daft. And what were James' parents thinking?! I suspect Jenner must have offered them money, but I haven't been able to find out if that's true. If you know the answer, please write and tell me!) He made a scratch on James's skin and rubbed the cowpox pus into it. He repeated this for a few days, and put in more pus each time. It won't surprise you to hear that James fell ill with cowpox, but he soon got better.

Jenner left James alone for six weeks, then got ready to carry out the really dangerous part of the experiment. This time, he got pus from someone with smallpox, and scratched it into James's arm the way he had done with the cowpox.

Then he waited.

If Jenner was right, catching cowpox would stop James from catching smallpox. He would be **immune** to it. If Jenner was wrong, James would get smallpox, and might well die, and his death would be Jenner's fault ...

So he waited.

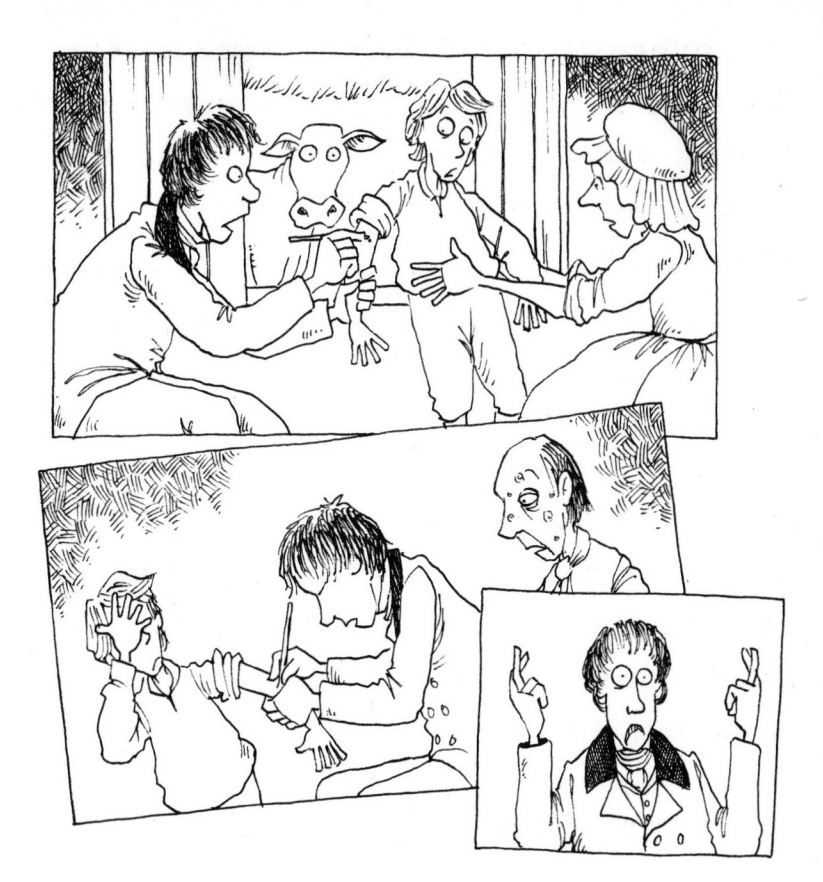

Luckily for James and Jenner, his idea was
right. James didn't get ill. He was now
immune to smallpox, and Jenner had
discovered something he called **vaccination**.
He chose the name because in Latin, which
was the language of science and learning in
those days, the word **vacca** means cow.

Jenner tried to get what he had found out published in scientific books. He was told he didn't have enough evidence that vaccination worked, so he vaccinated some more children, including his own baby son. None of them got smallpox.

Now, you would think people would be keen to be protected from such a terrible disease, but you'd be wrong. Many people laughed at Jenner's idea. There's a famous cartoon from the time that shows people being vaccinated and suddenly growing horns or hooves like a cow. As time went on though, the public slowly began to agree that vaccination was a good thing.

There's nothing in the history books about what happened to James or Sarah Nelmes, the milk maid, for the rest of their lives, but you can see the horns of Blossom the cow in the Jenner museum near Bristol!

The Science Bit ... Why Vaccination Works

The first time you meet a disease – chickenpox, for example – you get ill. Once you get better, you're not likely to get chickenpox again. You are now **immune** to it. But why do you get ill the first time? And what changes so that you don't get chickenpox again?

I need to tell you a bit about the immune system. This is what protects you against lots of diseases.

Your blood contains two sorts of cells, red and white. The red ones carry oxygen round your body. Your immune system is made of white blood cells, which come in different types. They travel in your blood, but some of them can also crawl out through gaps in the blood vessel walls. These ones wander all through your body, looking for things that shouldn't be there, and trying to destroy them. Different types of white blood cell have different ways of doing this.

Some of them eat up bacteria and viruses that have got into your body. Other white blood cells make special chemicals called **antibodies**.

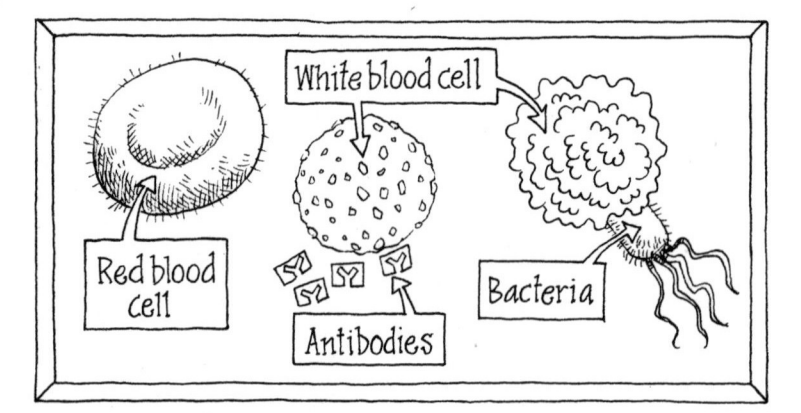

So how do these antibodies work?

All cells have 'markers' that stick out of their surface. These are called **antigens**. (Yes, I know it's confusing. Why can't they make the names more different?) Every cell in your body has antigens that identify it as part of you. (I always think of these as little flags with my name on them sticking out of my cells.) These tell your immune system not to attack them.

Anything that isn't part of you (like a chickenpox virus) has antigens that tell your immune system it shouldn't be there. (Like a little flag with 'chickenpox' on it.)

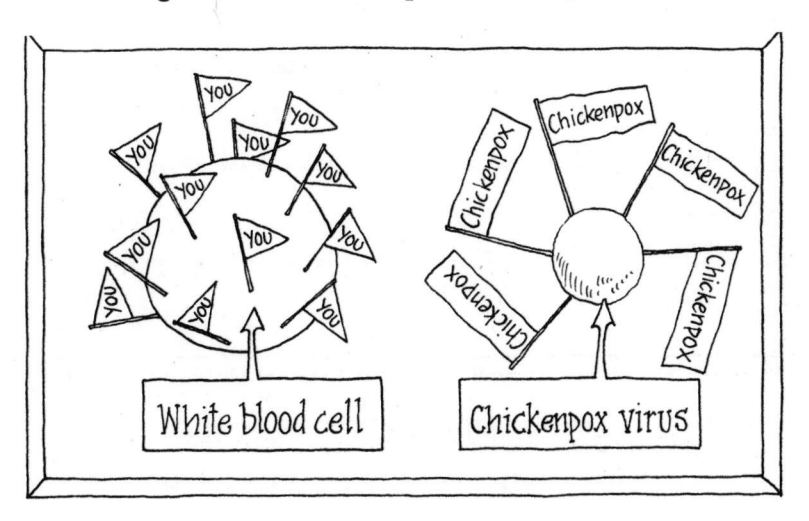

37

The white blood cells that make antibodies come in a huge number of different types. The antibody each type makes fits perfectly with one antigen, like a key fitting into a lock.

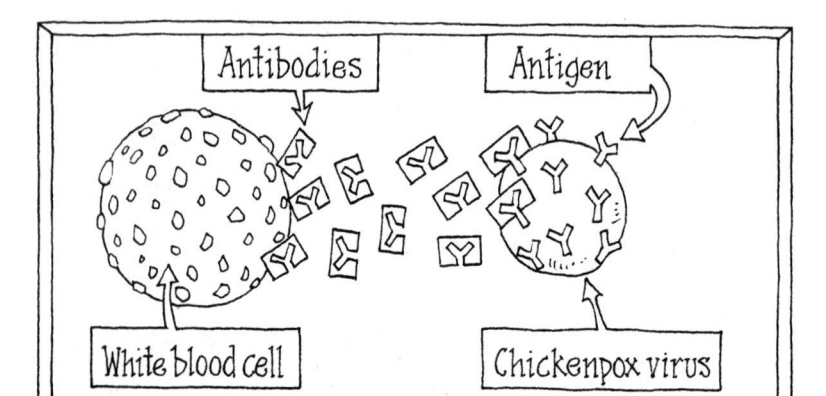

OK. Let's say some chickenpox viruses have got into your body, and you've never had chickenpox. Sooner or later, one of the viruses will bump into a white blood cell that makes the antibody to fit its antigen. When this happens, that white blood cell springs into action. It divides over and over so that there are lots of cells exactly like it, and they all start to make antibodies as fast as they can. The antibody glues the chickenpox viruses together and attracts other white blood cells to gobble them up. In the end, they make enough to kill all the viruses.

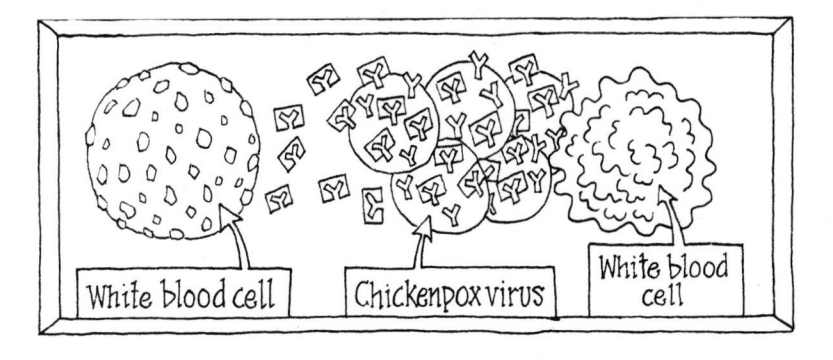

The only problem is, it's taken so long to get the system working that you are now covered in spots and look like a toad ... It takes a few days for the immune system to really get going, which is why you get ill. You see, the viruses have had plenty of time to get into lots of your cells and damage them.

The really clever part of the immune system is that it has a memory. Once it's met something like chickenpox once, it remembers which antibody it needs to make to get rid of it. To do this, it makes **memory cells**, which live for years. They float about in the blood, checking it all the time for (in this case) chickenpox. If they find some, the memory cells make antibodies so fast that you don't get ill at all.

In fact, this is going on all the time in your body. While you've been reading this, you've breathed in or swallowed thousands of germs, and most of them get zapped before they get the chance to do anything to you.

So, how does vaccination work?

It plays a trick on your immune system, and gets it ready to fight dangerous germs before it's met them. This means your body can deal with it before the germs have time to make you ill.

When you are vaccinated, you are injected with a tiny bit of the germ that causes the disease. This doesn't make you ill, because it's been killed or made weak. It still has its antigens though – the markers that tell your body they shouldn't be there. Your immune system leaps into action making antibodies, though you don't really need them at this point. The real purpose of the vaccination is to get your immune system to make memory cells, so that you can be protected against a serious disease without it making you ill first.

The reason Jenner's cowpox vaccination worked is that the antigens of cowpox and smallpox are so alike that the antibodies that knock out one will also destroy the other!

Vaccination Now

Most people in this country get vaccinated against lots of diseases. Here are just a few of them:

Polio	Tetanus
Diphtheria	Whooping Cough
Meningitis	Measles
Mumps	Rubella

You don't get vaccinated against smallpox, though your parents might have been, and your grandparents definitely would have been. There would be no point, because it doesn't exist any more. (Remember? We've killed that one off.)

If you go abroad, you might be vaccinated against some of these:

Yellow Fever	Typhoid
Cholera	Rabies
Hepatitis	Tuberculosis

Out of those ones, the one you least want to catch is rabies. If you get bitten by an animal with rabies and you haven't been vaccinated, doctors have to vaccinate you straight away. If that doesn't happen, you will certainly die. First you feel as if you've got flu, then you start to get confused. You can't swallow, and you see things that aren't there. You become terrified of water (yes, really!). After ten days or so, you die.

You won't get vaccinated against malaria because they've never been able to make a vaccine that works.

The Miracle Drug

In 1928 Professor Alexander Fleming went on holiday. Nice for him, but what's it got to do with this book? Wait and see ...

You may have been given antibiotics by the doctor sometimes. You take them for a few days, and if you've been given the right sort, you start to feel better. Antibiotics are drugs that kill bacteria. They're very good at that, but they can't kill viruses, so don't ask your doctor for them if you've got a cold, or flu, because they won't help.

But how were they found, and where do they come from?

Back to Professor Fleming's holiday ...

Fleming was working with bacteria that can cause sore throats. He grew them on a special jelly in glass dishes so that he could study them. When Fleming went on holiday some of these dishes got left out in his lab instead of being thrown away. When he came back, they had mould (a sort of green fungus) growing on them.

Fleming was about to throw them away when he saw that the bacteria nearest the mould had vanished. He began to wonder if the mould had made something that killed the bacteria.

Two weeks later...

He grew the mould in liquid, and tested the liquid on lots of different types of bacteria. He found that the liquid the mould had grown in could kill many of the bacteria, including ones that caused some human diseases. He called the substance that was killing the bacteria **penicillin**.

Next, he tried injecting mice with penicillin, to check it wouldn't harm them. Luckily, it didn't, but he did find that if you kept penicillin for very long, it didn't work any more.

What he should have done next was test penicillin on mice that had been infected by bacteria – but he got bored working with penicillin and moved on to something else.

Now, the next bit of this story should be that lots of scientists got very excited and spent all their time working out how to use penicillin.

Wrong!

No one was very interested.

It wasn't until 10 years later that two other scientists – called Howard Florey and Ernst Chain – got interested in Fleming's work. They injected mice with harmful bacteria, and gave some of the mice penicillin. Then they waited up all night to see what would happen ...

By morning, all the mice that hadn't been given penicillin were dead, and all the ones that had been given penicillin were fine.

When the Second World War started, Howard Florey and Ernst Chain thought penicillin might be important in treating injured soldiers. Many people thought England would soon be invaded by the German army. The scientists were worried that they might lose their penicillin if that happened, so they soaked their coats in it.

What??

It does make sense, really. Read on ...

When their coats dried out, the dried out mould was still on them. Mould can stay alive even when it's dry. All you have to do is put it in the right liquid, and it will start to grow again. Smart, or what?

The first person ever to be given penicillin was a policeman who had blood poisoning (which he had got from his toothbrush, believe it or not). He was very ill, but as soon as he was given the penicillin he started to get better. Sadly, they ran out of penicillin, and he died.

The race was on to find out how to make lots of penicillin. Remember, this was war time, and being able to treat wounds properly was very, very important. Florey and Chain flew to America and kept working there.

At last, they found a way to grow lots of the mould and get lots of penicillin, and they could start using it to treat people properly.

In 1945, Fleming, Florey and Chain were given the Nobel Prize for medicine. Penicillin was the first antibiotic. Since then, lots of other antibiotics have been discovered. They've saved millions of lives all over the world.

The trouble is, we've used them too much. This has let some of the bacteria become resistant to them. (This means the antibiotics can't kill them any more.) This is why you hear about 'superbugs' like MRSA in hospitals. These are bacteria that are very difficult to kill with antibiotics, and often kill the people who get them. It's a scary fact that more and more types of bacteria are getting resistant to antibiotics. What will we do if they stop working?

Chapter 4
The Future ...

Scientists are always trying to find new antibiotics, but it isn't easy. It takes 8-10 years and millions of pounds to get one through all the tests they have to do to check it's safe. The last one to pass was in 2005. This was 15 years after it had been discovered! There have only been 4 new antibiotics in the last 15 years. I'd always thought new ones were found quite regularly, but even though drug companies spend huge amounts of money looking, it's very hard to find one that kills bacteria but doesn't harm us. Don't panic though! There are other things to try...

Phage Medicine

I know, difficult to say, but phages are amazing once you know what they are. Phages are special viruses. They only attack bacteria. Every different type of bacteria gets attacked by some sort of phage, and this kills the bacteria.

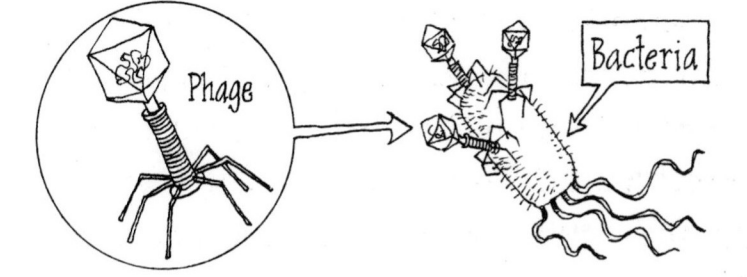

In Russia, they've used this fact to treat illnesses caused by bacteria for a long time. Now that antibiotics are becoming less useful, scientists in other countries are getting interested in phages too.

You can put them in a spray to kill bacteria on surfaces like tables and floors. You can make them into pills to kill bacteria inside people without harming them. Pretty useful!

Wallaby Milk

So strange that I had to put it in the book! A wallaby is a sort of small kangaroo. The milk that they make for their tiny babies contains a chemical that's 100 times better than penicillin at killing bacteria. Scientists in Australia think it could protect us against  'superbugs' like MRSA. These are bacteria that are really hard to kill with antibiotics. Now, I love to think of herds of wallabies being milked like cows, but sadly, this isn't going to happen. Instead, scientists hope to

make an artificial version of the special
chemical in the milk. Boring!

What Happens Next?

The quick answer is, I don't know, but that's not much of an answer.

• More and more bacteria are likely to get resistant to antibiotics. We'll have to be a lot more careful about how we use them.

• With any luck, some new antibiotics will be found. But don't count on it. Scientists have been looking very hard for a long time, and they haven't found many.

- We're getting better at making drugs that can help fight viruses. That's quite new. Up until the last few years, we couldn't treat diseases that were caused by viruses at all. This will be really important if Bird Flu does arrive.

- It's likely that we'll come up with vaccinations against some more diseases. As I was writing this, the government started using a new one that gives protection against a type of cancer.

- We might find better ways to kill the insects that pass on some of the germs that cause disease.

Phage medicine? Wallaby milk? Who knows what else might be found. The war against germs will never end. We'll never beat the germs. But hopefully, they'll never beat us either ...

AUTHOR CHECK LIST

Gill Arbuthnott

What's the most sick you have ever been?

I've been lucky. I've never been very sick. I think I can remember having the measles a long time ago which wasn't very nice, and I had proper flu once which was horrible – people who tell you they have flu and are still on their feet just have a cold!

What illness would you like to invent a cure for?

It's not really an illness but I'd like to invent a cure for being lazy. One thing that I can't stand is people who say, "I could do that if only I had the time ..." Almost everyone does have the time to do something if they really want to do it.

If you were ill, who would you least like to operate on you?

My cat? No – wait – anyone who's had me as their Biology teacher. Lying on the operating table and hearing someone say, "Hello, Miss, remember me?" is not something I want to find happening to me.

Which experiment would you like to carry out?

I'd quite like to try and breed a cat that could fly, but then of course I'd have to breed mice that could fly for the cat to chase ...

Barrington Stoke would like to thank all its readers for commenting on the manuscript before publication and in particular:

Francesca Burns
Josephine Cox
Emma Duffy
Laura Ann Hamilton
Laurence Kerr
Declan McVeigh
Nikita More

Become a Consultant!

Would you like to give us feedback on our titles before they are published? Contact us at the email address below – we'd love to hear from you!

info@barringtonstoke.co.uk
www.barringtonstoke.co.uk

ILLUSTRATOR CHECK LIST

Mike Phillips

What's the most sick you have ever been?

I was never ill when I was young. When I was 36, however, I caught chickenpox from my children. They thought it was very funny. I didn't – I was in bed for a week!

What illness would you like to invent a cure for?

I wish I could invent a cure for sadness. I hate being sad.

If you were ill, who would you least like to operate on you?

A horse. Hooves are useless for tricky operations.

Which illness do you hope you never get?

I don't want to get any!!

Which experiment would you like to carry out?

I'd like to find out how many ring doughnuts I would have to eat before I lost my love for them! Yum!

Try another book in the
REALITY CHECK
series

Crazy Creatures
by Gill Arbuthnott

Mad Scientists
by Gill Arbuthnott

Snow Tigers
by Simon Chapman

The Last Duel
by Martyn Beardsley

Escape From Colditz
by Deborah Chancellor